Christmas

by Natalie M. Rosinsky

Content Adviser: Dr. Alexa Sandmann, Professor of Literacy,
The University of Toledo; Member, National Council for the Social Studies

Reading Adviser: Dr. Linda D. Labbo, Department of Reading Education,
College of Education, The University of Georgia

Let's See Library
Compass Point Books
Minneapolis, Minnesota

Compass Point Books
3722 West 50th Street, #115
Minneapolis, MN 55410

Visit Compass Point Books on the Internet at *www.compasspointbooks.com* or e-mail your
request to *custserv@compasspointbooks.com*

Cover: Christmas wreath

Photographs ©: Dianne Dietrich Leis, cover; Arte & Immagini srl/Corbis, 4; North Wind Picture Archives, 6, 10;
Unicorn Stock Photos/Martha McBride, 8; Unicorn Stock Photos/Andre Jenny, 12; Unicorn Stock Photos/Aneal
Vohra, 14; Unicorn Stock Photos/Nancy Ferguson, 16; Digital Stock, 18; Reuters NewMedia Inc./Corbis, 20;
John Cross/The Free Press, 24.

Editor: Catherine Neitge
Photo Researcher: Svetlana Zhurkina
Photo Selector: Catherine Neitge
Designer: Melissa Voda

Library of Congress Cataloging-in-Publication Data
Rosinsky, Natalie M. (Natalie Myra)
    Christmas / by Natalie M. Rosinsky; reading adviser, Linda D. Labbo.
        v. cm.— (Let's see library)
    Includes bibliographical references and index.
    Contents: What is Christmas?—How did Christmas begin?—What is most important at Christmas?—Who
brings gifts at Christmas?—How are trees and greenery part of Christmas?—How else is Christmas
observed?—How has Christmas changed?—How is Christmas observed in the United States?—How is Christmas
observed around the world?
    ISBN 0-7565-0389-2 (hardcover)
    1. Christmas—Juvenile literature. [1. Christmas. 2. Holidays.] I. Title. II. Series.
    GT4985.5 .R67 2002
    394.2663—dc21   2002003041

Table of Contents

What Is Christmas?

Christmas is a time of joy. It is part of the Christian religion. Every December 25, most Christians observe the birthday of Jesus Christ. Christians believe that Jesus is the son of God.

The story of Jesus is 2,000 years old. It took place in the country we now call Israel. Jesus's parents on Earth were Mary and Joseph. They were traveling and had no place to stay. Jesus was born in a **stable** in Bethlehem. Animals and birds watched over him. Wise men brought him gifts.

◄ This painting from the sixteenth century shows the baby Jesus in the stable. It was painted by an assistant to Michelangelo.

How Did Christmas Begin?

Winter days can be dark and gloomy. Many older religions already had winter holidays to welcome light. Christians believed that Jesus was "the light of the world." A shining star had led the wise men to baby Jesus in Bethlehem. No one knew the exact birthday of Jesus. It made sense to observe his birthday during winter.

In the fourth century, December 25 became Christmas for most Christians. Glowing candles were one Christmas idea taken from older winter holidays.

◄ *The wise men followed a shining star to Bethlehem, where Jesus was born.*

What Is Most Important at Christmas?

Going to church is a special way of observing Jesus's birth. It is even part of this holiday's name. *Mass* means "church service" in **Latin**.

Some churches and homes are decorated with **nativity** figures. Long ago, many people could not read. They learned about Christmas by seeing who was at the stable. Sometimes, people stage the story of Jesus, Mary, and Joseph.

The wise men brought gifts to the baby Jesus. At Christmas, many people give presents to their family and friends. People often give gifts to the poor, too.

◄ *Nativity figures portray the first Christmas in Bethlehem.*

Who Brings Gifts at Christmas?

Many children believe that someone special also brings them gifts. In the United States, this is Santa Claus. In Germany, this is the Christ child. In Mexico, it is the wise men who bring gifts. In Italy, the magical gift-giver is an old lady.

Santa Claus is famous! Sometimes, he is called good Saint Nick. Saint Nicholas was a real person who helped others. Saint Nicholas lived in the fourth century. People say he once threw gold coins down a chimney. The coins fell into shoes and socks near the fireplace. This is why people began to hang up stockings at Christmas.

◄ *Santa Claus was first pictured as this plump, jolly old man by American artist Thomas Nast in the 1860s.*

How Are Trees and Greenery Part of Christmas?

Trees were also part of older winter holidays. Bright **evergreens** reminded people of spring.

Christmas trees were first decorated in Germany in the early 1600s. Candles, fruit, and nuts were used to decorate fir trees. In the nineteenth century, Christmas trees became popular in England and the United States. Today's trees often have fancy decorations. Indoor and outdoor trees shine with bright, electric lights.

Other greenery is also part of Christmas. People hang **holly** and evergreen wreaths and branches. They even kiss under the **mistletoe!**

◄ A tree glows with bright lights in front of a Vermont library.

How Else Is Christmas Observed?

Many people have feasts on Christmas. Turkey is a popular Christmas food in the United States. Some people share or give food to people in need, too. These ideas have been part of Christmas since it began.

Some people decorate their homes and businesses. They may use bells, the star of Bethlehem, or Santa figures. The green of trees and the red of berries are common Christmas colors.

Singing Christmas carols is fun! Some carols tell the story of Jesus. Other carols are about Santa Claus or winter.

◄ Costumed carolers sing Christmas songs in Kansas City.

How Has Christmas Changed?

Christians have found other ways to observe Christmas. An old story from Mexico tells about a poor girl. She only had weeds to offer Mary, the mother of Jesus. The weeds grew bright red, star-shaped flowers! This popular Christmas plant is called the poinsettia. It is named after Joel R. Poinsett. More than 150 years ago, he brought the plant to the United States from Mexico.

Sending Christmas cards is another Christmas practice. Cards first appeared in England in the 1840s. People in the United States started sending Christmas cards about 1875.

◀ The colorful poinsettia is named after Joel R. Poinsett.

How Is Christmas Observed in the United States?

Christmas is a national holiday in the United States. Schools, government offices, and businesses are closed. Many offices and businesses close early on December 24, Christmas Eve. The holiday season lasts until January 1, New Year's Day.

Each December, the president lights the national Christmas tree. It is a living tree that stands in front of the White House. The government also prints Christmas stamps.

In some cities, Mexican-Americans act out the journey of Mary and Joseph. They do this for nine nights. It is called *Las Posadas*.

◄ The national Christmas tree glows with lights near the White House.

How Is Christmas Observed Around the World?

The Christmas season changes in different countries. It begins as early as December 6. This is St. Nicholas Day in the Netherlands. The season lasts as long as January 13. This is when Christmas trees are put away in Sweden.

January 6 is called Three Kings' Day in Spain and Mexico. It is important to children. It is the day they get presents! January 6 is also known as Epiphany or Twelfth Day. It is twelve days after Christmas. January 5, the eve of Epiphany, is called Twelfth Night. In England, the Christmas season lasts until Twelfth Night.

◄ *Actors portray the wise men during Three Kings' Day festivities in Mexico City.*

Glossary

evergreens—trees, plants, or shrubs that have green leaves or needles all year long

holly—an evergreen plant usually having shiny pointed leaves and bright red berries

Latin—the language Christians used for prayers and early Romans spoke

mistletoe—a green plant with small white berries

nativity—the Latin word for birth, often used for the birth of Jesus

stable—a building where farm animals are kept and fed

Did You Know?

• Some Christians observe Christmas on January 6. These people belong to the Russian or Greek Orthodox branches of Christianity.

• Santa Claus did not always use reindeer. Long ago, he rode a horse, donkey, or even a goat!

• Electric lights first decorated a Christmas tree in 1882. This tree belonged to a friend of Thomas Edison. Edison had recently invented the light bulb.

Want to Know More?

In the Library

Cooney, Barbara. *The Story of Christmas*. New York: HarperCollins, 1995.

Giblin, James Cross. *The Truth About Santa Claus*. New York: Thomas Y. Crowell, 1985.

Hoyt-Goldsmith, Diane. *Las Posadas: An Hispanic Christmas Celebration*. New York: Holiday House, 1999.

Lankford, Mary D. *Christmas Around the World*. New York: Morrow, 1995.

On the Web

Not Just for Kids! Christmas
http://www.night.net/christmas
For Christmas music, stories, crafts, and recipes

Christmas Pageant of Peace
http://www.nps.gov/whho/pageant
For information about the national Christmas tree in Washington, D.C.

National Christmas Tree Association
http://realchristmastrees.org
For games, fun facts about Christmas trees, and how the White House tree is chosen

Through the Mail

Embassy of Finland
3301 Massachusetts Ave., N.W.
Washington, DC 20008
For information about Turku, which is known as the Christmas City of Finland

On the Road

King's Canyon National Park
Sanger, California 93657
To see a 267-foot (81-meter) tall sequoia tree known as the Nation's Christmas Tree. It is also called the General Grant Tree. This tree honors people who have died for the United States.

Index

About the Author

Natalie M. Rosinsky writes about history, science, and other fun things. One of her two cats usually sits on her computer as she works in Mankato, Minnesota. Both cats pay close attention as she and her family make and eat special holiday foods. Natalie earned graduate degrees from the University of Wisconsin and has been a high school and college teacher.